Naming Your Pet

Naming Your Pet

Mary Helen Detrick and
Nancy Butler White

Illustrated by
Nancy Butler White

ARCO PUBLISHING COMPANY, INC.
NEW YORK

Published by Arco Publishing Company, Inc.
219 Park Avenue South, New York, N.Y. 10003

Library of Congress Cataloging in Publication Data

Detrick, Mary Helen
  Naming your pet.

  1. Pets—Names.   I.   White, Nancy Butler, joint
author.   II.   Title.

SF411.3.D47   636   77-22065
ISBN 0-668-04397-0 (Library Edition)
ISBN 0-668-04401-2 (Paper Edition)

Printed in the United States of America

To
Gary Carlson, D.V.M.
and
Erasmus

CONTENTS

INTRODUCTION

How does one choose a name for a pet?

Some people like to choose a name based on the physical characteristics of the pet—"Spot," or "Whitey," or "Stubby." Others choose a contemporary name, often one popularized by a currently popular sports figure, politician, or comic strip character: "Yogi," or "Jimmy," or "Snoopy," for example. While there is nothing wrong with any of these naming techniques, wouldn't it be better to customize your pet's name? To give it a name which reflects the personality of the animal (or bird, or fish, or reptile)? Perhaps, too, a name can come from the pet's heritage, or refer to the locale from which its ancestors sprung.

Though naming a pet is a fun project, it's worth your time to think before deciding on a name. If you place the handle of "Bozo" or "Puss" or "Chip" too quickly on your pet, the poor victim may have to endure a lifetime of suffering and scorn at the hands of snickering peers whose owners had enough concern to choose their names with loving care.

This little book will not tell you what to name your pet, but in it you will find a houseful of suggestions listed from A to Z. Some have traditional definitions and meanings. Other names reflect the interpretations or the imaginations of the authors. Chances are very good that one certain name will strike your fancy. It will fit neatly with your pet's personality—or smile. Or maybe it will "sound just like him."

Happy naming to you and your new friend. And when he asks, and he will, don't be afraid to tell him that you custom-selected his name from this little book. Then your pet will know that you cared enough to name him the very best.

FEMALE NAMES

A

ABBY—gentle
ABIGAIL—joyful
   (Abbie)
ADA—happy
ADELINE—musical
   (Addie)
ADELPHE—beloved sister
   (Adele, Del)
ADONICA—sweet
ADORE—bittersweet
ADRIENNE—dark
   (Adriane, Adriana)
AGATHA—good
AGGIE—sacred, pure
AGNES—revered
AILEEN—lighthearted
AIMÉE—beloved
ALABASTER—prized, delicate
ALARICE—leader
ALBA—noble, bright
ALBERTA—honorable
ALDA—good spirits
ALDORA—guardian
ALEXA—cooperative
ALEXANDRA—considerate
   (Alex, Sandy)
ALEXINA—resourceful
   (Alexine)

ALEXIS—companionable
ALFREDA—farseeing
ALICE—cheerful
    (Alicia, Alisa, Alyce, Alys)
ALICIA—good-natured
ALISON—fiery
ALLEGRA—sprite
ALMA—kindly
ALMIRA—exalted
ALOYSIA—instigator
    (Aloyse)
ALPHA—good beginning
ALPHONSINE—feisty
    (Alfie)
ALTA—tall
ALTHEA—wholesome
ALVA—white
ALVINA—beloved
AMABEL—lovable
    (Amy)
AMANDA—easygoing
AMARYLLIS—delicate
AMAZON—large, strong
AMBER—gemlike
AMBROSIA—immortal
AMBROSINE—delectable
    (Ambrosina)
AMELIA—worker
AMETHYST—gemstone
AMITY—friendly
AMY—dainty
ANASTASIA—aristocratic

Amanda & George

ANCHOVY—delectable
ANDREA—sporty
    (Andrina)
ANDROMEDA—sylphe
ANGEL—angelic
    (Angela, Angelina)
ANGIE—happy
ANITA—graceful
ANN—saintly
    (Anne, Anna, Annie)
ANNABEL—joy
    (Annabelle)
ANTHEA—flowery
ANTOINETTE—inestimable
    (Tonie, Tony)
ANTONIA—valuable
APHRODITE—goddess of love
APPLE—choicest
APRICOT—delicious
APRIL—reborn
ARABELLA—heroine, courageous
    (Arabelle)
ARDELLE—zealous
ARLENE—ardent
ARTEMIS—Greek goddess, gifted
    (Artie)
ARTIS—beautiful
ASTARTE—goddess of fertility
ASTER—flowerlike
ASTOR—bright yellow
ASTRID—impulsive
ATHENA—wisdom

ATLANTA—seaworthy
AUDREY—noble
AUGUSTA—majestic
AURA—feathery
AURORA—dawn
AVA—birdlike
AVELINE—hazel
AVIS—flighty
AZALEA—special choice
AZTEC—tawny

Bruno

Joe

Beloved, Belle

B

BABA—self-sufficient
BABE—small
   (Baby)
BABETTE—alone
BABS—newcomer
BANGLES—decorative
BAPTISTA—pure
BARBARA—unique
   (Barb, Barby, Barbie)
BATHSHEBA—loyal
BEATRICE—blessed
   (Beatrix, Bea, Trixie)
BEAUTY—joy
BECKY—old-fashioned
BEE-BEE—bright
BEGONIA—show-off
BELINDA—willowy
BELLA—beautiful
   (Belle)
BELOVED—very loved
BENITA—glorify
BERNADETTE—favored
BERNADINE—staunch
BERNICE—victorious
BERNITA—steadfast
   (Bernette)
BERTIE—cajoler

BERYL—jewel-like
BESS—humble
   (Bessie)
BETH—domesticated
BETSY—chaste
BETTE—serene
BETTINA—adoring
BETTY—pure
BEULAH—comfortable
BEVERLY—adaptable
BIANCA—white, fair
BIDDY—cheerful
BIJOU—amiable
BITTY—tiny one
BLANCHE—white, fair
BLENDA—easygoing
BLONDIE—fair-haired
BLOSSOM—springy
BLYTHE—happy
BOBEE—frivolous
BOBO—clever
BON BON—sweet
BONITA—good
BONNIBELLE—good, beautiful
BONNIE—good
BONUS—extra special
BOO—rambunctious
BOOTS—swift footed
BO-PEEP—youthful
BOUFFANT—puffy
BOW—neat, tidy
BREEZIE—windy

BRENDA—sharp
BRIDGET—strong
BRINDLE—prim
BRUNELLE—intelligent
BRUNHILDA—very active
BRYNHILDE—strong
BUBBLES—lively
BUENA—good
BUNNY—soft
BURNETTA—little brown one
BUTTERCUP—springy, yellow
BUTTERSCOTCH—creamy rich color

C

CACTUS—hardy, prickly
CALAMITY—trouble
CALLISTA—beautiful
   (Calli)
CAMEO—ivory, serene
CAMILLA—graceful
CAMILLE—beauty
CANDACE—flowing
   (Candy)
CANDIDA—white
CANDY—sweet
CAPRICORN—heavenly
CARA—friend
CARAMEL—charmer
CARAS—friendly
CAREME—pleasing
CARESSA—lovable
CARIA—whisper
CARISSA—creative
CARLA—easygoing
CARLITA—little woman
CARLOTTA—regal
CARMA—destiny
CARMEL—earthy
CARMEN—rosy
CARO—joyful
CAROL—song of joy

CAROLINE—very feminine
CARRIE—resourceful
CASS—helpful
    (Cassey, Cassie)
CASSANDRA—agreeable
CASSIE—bubbly
CATHERINE—gentle-hearted
CATHLEEN—unblemished
CATRINA—graceful
CECELIA—hazy
CELESTE—godly
CELESTINE—heavenly
CELIA—stimulating
CELLA—tempestuous
CERA—certitude
CEREBUS—cloudlike
CERES—mythlike
CHA-CHA—prancer
CHAMOIS—soft
    (Chammy, Shammy)
CHAMPAGNE—costly, bubbly
CHARIS—loving
    (Charissa)
CHARITY—kind
CHARLENE—chatty
CHARLOTTE—thoughtful
    (Char, Lottie)
CHARMAINE—charming
    (Charmer)
CHATTY—talkative
CHELSEA—alluring
CHERI—dearest

CHERISE—slinky
CHERRY—considerate
CHERUB—innocent, lovely
CHI-CHI—sphinxlike
CHIFFON—downy light
CHINTZ—colorful
CHIQUITA—saucy
CHLOE—blooming
CHRISTABELLE—fair
CHRISTEL—brave
CHRISTINA—integrity
CHRISTINE—virtuous
CHUBBY—plump
CIMONE—attentive
CINDER—ashes, charcoal
CINDERELLA—princess
CINTHIE—sweet
CIRCE—siren
CLAIRE—bright, illustrious
    (Clara, Clarabelle)
CLARICE—famous
CLARINDA—bright, fair
CLAUDETTE—weak
CLAUDIA—frail
CLEMATIS—clinging
CLEMENTINE—merciful
    (Clemmie)
CLEO—famous
CLEOPATRA—proud, haughty
CLORINDA—renown
CLOTHILDA—feisty

CLOVER—blossom, lucky
   (Cluny)
COCOA—mellow
COLETTE—victorious
COLLEEN—ladylike
COLUMBIA—dove
COLUMBINE—climber
CON—little
CONCHA—shell-like
CONCHITA—saucy
CONCITA—successful
CONCORDIA—old-fashioned
CONSTANCE—steady
   (Con, Connie)
CONSUELO—sorrowful
COOKIE—sweet
COPIA—overflowing
COPPER—shiny
COQUETTE—flirty
CORA—maiden
CORAL—blushing
CORETA—ancient
CORINNE—maidenly
   (Corinna)
CORKY—springy
CORNELIA—heavenly
COUNTESS—aristocrat
CRABBY—irritable
CRACKERS—crunchy
CREEPER—slinky
CREEPY—clever

CRICKET—jumpy
CROCUS—spring flower
CRYSTAL—clear
CUDDLES—affectionate, lovable
CUPCAKE—small, dainty
CUPID—goddess of love
    (Love-Bug)
CURLY—ringlets and waves
CYBELLE—florid
CYCLONE—whirlwind
CYNTHIA—hunter
    (Cynthie)

D

DAFFODIL—spring bloom, yellow
  (Daffy)
DAFFY—foolish
DAGMAR—pompous
DAHLIA—flowerlike
DAINTRY—warmth
DAINTY—delicate
DAISY—first-rate
DALLY—playful
DAMA—refined, gentle
DAMARIS—gentle
DAME—ladylike
DANDELION—sunny
DANDY—stylish, primper
DANIELLA—self-sufficient
DANITA—trustful
DAPHENE—glossy, showy
  (Daphne)
DARA—bold, wise
DARCY—protective
DARIA—queenly
DARICE—regal
DARLENE—tender, loving
DARLING—beloved
DARYL—very dear
DAUPHINE—royal
DAVIDA—beloved

27

DAWN—fresh, understanding
DEANNA—bright as day
DEBBY—domestic
DEBORAH—flighty
DEDE—swift
DEIRDRE—bright-eyed
DELIA—solitary
DELICIA—delightful
DELIGHT—pleasurable
DELILAH—gentle, tender
DELLA—youthful
DELMA—nymphlike
DELPHE—calm, serene
DELPHINE—temperate
DELTA—friendly
DEMETRIA—fertility
DEMURE—coy
DENA—colorful
DENISE—mellow
DESIRÉE—desired
DESMA—trustworthy
DESTINY—fortunate
DEVIL—tempter, scalawag
DIAMOND—sparkling
DIANA—goddess of moon and hunt
DIANE—bright, shiny
DIANTHA—supreme
DIGNA—dignified
DILLY—silly, daffy
DIMITY—dainty
DINA—pleasant, decisive
DINAH—authoritative

DING-A-LING—silly
DIRCE—siren, alluring
DIXIE—free spirit
DIZZY—foolish, silly, giddy
DODIE—delicate
DOLLY—special
DOLORES—sorrowful
DOMINIQUE—heavenly
DONATA—generous, sharing
DONCELLA—maidenly
DONNA—ladylike
DOPEY—sleepy
DORA—giving, friendly
DORCAS—graceful
DORINDA—bountiful
DORIS—nymphlike
DOROTHY—ethereal
   (Dot, Dottie)
DORUS—talented
DOVE—gentle
DREAMY—soft-eyed
DRU—strong
DRUSILLA—intense
DUCHESS—aristocratic
DUCKY—dandy
DULCY—sweet
DUMPLING—favorite
DUMPY—plump
DUSTY—powdery

E

EASTER—dawn, spring
EBBA—echo, return
ECHO—melodious
ECSTASY—rapture, joy
    (Stacy)
EDA—prosperous
EDELINA—simple
EDIE—valuable
EDITH—costly
EDMUNDA—protective
EDNA—tiny, small
EDWARDINE—defensive
    (Edwina, Edie, Dina)
EFFIE—famous
EGBERTA—glowing
EILEEN—luminous
ELAINE—sunny
    (Laney)
ELBERTA—noble, bright
ELEANOR—gleaming
ELECTRA—bright, shiny
ELFIN—fairylike
ELFREDA—befriender
ELISE—solemn, maidenly
ELISSA—truthful
ELIZA—reverent
ELIZABETH—faithful, loving

ELLA—elfin
ELLEN—gentle
(Ellie)
ELMA—amiable
ELMIRA—distinguished
ELNORA—roguish
ELOISE—eminent, prominent
ELRICA—quiet
ELSPETH—adoring
ELVINA—tenacious
ELVIRA—fair
EMELINE—busybee
EMERALD—green-eyed
EMILY—builder
EMMA—protective
(Emmy)
EMOGENE—childlike
ENDORA—imitative
ENID—spotless
ENRICA—domestic
EPSILON—small, fifth
ERASMA—friendly
ERICA—noble, lordly
ERIS—fragrant
ERLINE—trustworthy
ERMA—stately
ERMINA—splendid
ERNA—willful
ERNESTINE—grave, serious
(Ernie)
ESME—jewel-like
ESMERALDA—gemlike, sparkling

ESSIE—attention seeker
ESTELLE—starlike
ESTHER—special
ESTRELLA—favorite
ETHEL—royal
ETNA—explosive, temperamental
ETTA—little
   (Ettie)
EUGENIA—aristocrat
EULALIA—gentle
EUNICE—victorious
EUPHEMIA—renown
EUSTACIA—dependable
EVA—soulful
EVANGELINE—joyful
EVE—lively
EVELYN—pleasant
EVIE—faithful

F

FABIA—lovely
FAITH—hope, trust
FANCY—dreamy, fastidious
FANFARE—showy, noisy
FANNY—carefree
FANTASIA—fantasy
FARA—exotic
FARRAH—exceptional
FAUNA—delicate, wispy
FAWN—young deer, swift
FAY—fairy, elf
FEATHER—light, soft, frivolous
FEDORA—beloved
FELICE—happy
FELICIA—joyful
FELIPA—horse-lover
FERN—feathery
FIDELIA—faithful, truthful
    (Fidelity)
FIFI—fluffy
FIFINE—catlike
FILLY—young and wild
FIREFLY—bright, soft
FLAME—excited, emotional
FLAPPER—courageous
FLAVIA—yellowish
FLOPPY—long-eared, flabby

FLOPSY—flexible
FLORA—seed-picker
FLORENCE—thriving
FLORETTA—vigorous
FLORIDA—healthy
  (Florina)
FLOSSY—luxuriant
  (Flossie)
FLOWER—bud, sweetness
FLOYCE—ostentatious
FLUFFY—downy
  (Fluff)
FOLLY—foolish
FONDA—serious
FORTUNA—fortunate
FOXY—sylph
FRANCES—free spirit
FRANCHETTE—self-reliant
FRANCHON—coquette
FRANCINE—independent
  (Francie)
FRECKLES—spotted, sun worshipper
FRIEDA—peaceful
FRIENDLY—loving
FRISKY—frolicky
FRITZI—peaceful
FROSTY—calm, cool
FRU-FRU—frills, adornments
FULVIA—yellow
FUNNYFACE—jovial
FURRY—hairy, shaggy

G

GABBY—talkative
GABRIELLE—courageous
GAIETY—cheerful, merry
GAIL—gay, happy
GALATEA—milky white
GALE—happy-go-lucky
GARDA—sturdy
GARDENIA—fragrant
GARLAND—legendary
GARNET—radiant
GAY—happy
GAZELLE—nimble
GEM—precious
GEMINI—twins
GENEVA—juniper
GENEVIEVE—undulating
GENIE—magical
GEORGETTE—earthy
GERALDINE—youthful
GERANIUM—aromatic
GERDA—protective
GERTRUDE—maternal
GIDGET—little, small
GIGI—fanciful
GILBERTINA—honorable
GILDA—adoring
GIMLET—hole digger

GINA—free spirit
GINGER—spicy
   (Gin, Ginny)
GLADYS—joyful
GLAMOUR—bewitching, captivating
GLENDA—rejoice
GLENNA—recluse
GLORIA—glorious
GLORY—heavenly
GLOWWORM—luminous
GODIVA—independent
GO-GO—dancer
GOLDENROD—vivid
GOLDIE—golden-haired
GRACE—appreciative, thoughtful
GRACEFUL—elegant
GRACIA—graceful
GRANITE—stubborn
GREEDY—gluttonous
GRETA—white, smooth
GRETCHEN—little pearl
GRETEL—youthful
GRISELDA—persistant
GRISSEL—obstinate, stubborn
GRITS—southern delight
GUINEVERE—fairy lady
GUSSIE—athletic
GWENDOLYN—aristocratic
   (Gwyn)
GYPSY—nomad, wanderer

H

HAIDEE—modest
HALLIE—lovable
HANNAH—graceful
   (Hana)
HAPPINESS—joy
   (Happy)
HARMONY—agreeable, peaceable
HATTIE—successful
HAZEL—easygoing
HEATHER—colorful
HEBE—youthful
HEDDA—prissy
HEDIA—pleasing
HEDWIG—protector
HEDY—conformable
HEIDI—modest
HELEN—intelligent
HELENUS—statuesque
HELGA—awesome
HELOISE—heroic
HELSA—devoted
HENRIETTA—domestic
HENRIKA—humble
HEPHZIBAH—delightful
   (Hepsy)
HERA—ladylike
HERMERA—worldly

HERMIONE—earthly
HESTER—heavenly
HIGHNESS—purebred, haughty
HILARY—cheerful
   (Hilaria)
HILDA—brave
HILDEGARDE—protective
HILDRETH—helpful
HILDY—pugnacious
HILMA—organizer
HOLLY—jolly, bright
HOMINY—grits
HONEY—sweet
HONEYBEE—sweet, lively
HONOR—integrity
   (Honoria)
HOPE—trustworthy
HOPPY—flighty
HORTENSE—digger
HURRICANE—whirlwind
HYACINTH—blue-eyed

I

IANTHE—prudent
IBBY—sensible
IDA—happy, cheerful
IDALINE—content
IDELLA—blissful
IDLE—lazy
IDONA—industrious
IGNACIA—fiery
ILEANA—stubborn
ILIA—poetic
ILKA—suave
ILONA—dawn
ILSA—imaginative
IMAGE—likeness
IMOGENE—look alike
IMPERIAL—magnificent, superior
INA—considerate
INDEPENDENCE—self-reliant
INEZ—thoughtful
INGRID—daughter
INNOCENT—harmless
IRENE—peaceful
IRIS—Greek goddess
IRMA—noble
ISA—staunch
ISABELLA—idolizer
ISIDORA—moonstruck

ISIS—moon goddess
ISOLDE—fair, temperate
ITHECA—pantherlike
IVY—clinging

J

JACALYN—gracious
JACINTH—cheerful, bright, blooming
    (Jacintha)
JACQUELINE—supplanter
JADE—envious
JAM—sticky, messy
JAMA—daughter
JANA—gracious
JANE—benevolent
    (Janet)
JANETTE—devout
JANICE—loyal
    (Janus)
JANUARY—starter
JASMINE—exotic
JEAN—pretty
    (Jeanette, Jeannie)
JELLY—slithery
JENNIFER—wavy form
    (Jen, Jenny)
JESSICA—long-haired
    (Jessie)
JEWEL—precious
JILL—sweetheart
JINGLE—noisy
JOAN—courteous, polite
JOBINA—desire

JOCELYN—merry, jovial
JOCOBINA—schemer
JOHANNA—talented
JOLETTA—colorful
JONEA—famous
JONELLA—dovelike
JOSEPHA—prolific
    (Josie)
JOSEPHINE—imperial
JOY—conviviality, merry
JUANITA—generous
JUDITH—praised
    (Judy)
JULIA—youthful
    (Julie)
JULIET—Romeo's lady, sweetheart
JUNE—warmth, happiness
JUNE-BUG—whimsical, springlike
JUSTINE—true and just

K

KAREN—unselfish
KARLA—tomboy
KARMA—decisive
KATHERINE—sure and true
    (Kathie, Katie)
KATHLEEN—thoughtful
    (Kathie)
KATRINA—regal
KATRINKA—innocent, chaste
KAY—virtuous
KEEPSAKE—memento
KIM—faultless
KIRSTEN—kindness, love
KIT—follower
KITTLE—kittenish
KITTY—purr-plexed
KOKO—frivolous
KOREN—maidenly
KRINKLE—hefty
KRISTINA—majestic

L

LACY—delicate
LADY—titled, feminine
LADYBIRD—do-gooder
LADYBUG—good luck
LAIKA—traveler
LALA—tulip
LALITA—artless
LAMPKIN—softness
LANA—light
LANETTE—solitary
LA PASIONARIA—passion flower
LARA—famous
LARINE—sea gull
LARISSA—cheerful
LAURA—victorious
LAUREL—a winner
    (Laurie)
LAURENA—courageous
LAVINIA—champion
LAZY—idle
LEAH—weary
    (Lee)
LEANDER—flimsy
LEDA—sluggish
    (Lee)
LEILA—dark, murky
LENA—light

44

LENORA—lighthearted
    (Lena, Lora)
LENORE—lighthearted
LEONA—shaggy
LEONARDA—lionlike, mangy
LESLIE—homemaker
LETA—gay-spirited
LETITIA—joyful
    (Letty, Tish)
LEXINE—benevolent
LIANE—agreeable
LIBBY—chubby
LIBERTY—staunch, true
    (Bert)
LIDIA—majestic
LILAC—blooming, bushy
LILIAS—slender, delicate
LILITH—demon
LILLIAN—truthful
LILY—showy, delicate
LINA—abrupt
LINDA—beautiful
LINDY—southern belle
LINETTE—graceful
LISA—willowy
LISBETH—particular, fussy
LISE—curvacious
LISETTE—coquette
LISI—charmer
LITTLE-ONE—endearing
LIVIA—drab
LIZA—twinkle

LIZABETH—dainty
(Lizabet)
LIZZIE—drudge
LOIS—haughty
LOLA—earthy
LOLANDA—limpid
LOLITA—slinky
LOLLY—jolly
LOLLY-ANN—petite
LORA—alluring
LORELEI—siren
LORELLE—fortitude
LORENA—brave, courageous
LORETTA—tenacious
LORI—swift
LORINDA—fearless
LORIS—coy, shy
LORNA—spirited
LORRAINE—valorous
LOTTA—plucky
(Lottie)
LOTUS—dreamy
LOUELLA—chatterer
LOUISE—champion, defender
(Lou, Louisa, Lisa)
LOVERLY—cuddly, affectionate
LUCELLA—lighthearted, carefree
LUCIA—nonchalant
LUCILLE—happy-go-lucky
(Luci, Lucy, Lucinda, Cindy)
LUCKY—fortunate
LUCRETIA—frivolous

Lotus & Thalia

LUCY—happy-go-lucky
LUDMILLA—beloved
   (Luddie)
LUGENE—aristocratic
LULIE—swift-footed
LULU—wolfish
LUNA—moon
LUPE—brilliant
LUZETTE—shimmering
LYCIA—contented
LYDIA—haughty
LYNNE—sylph
LYRE—melodious
LYSANDRA—liberator

M

MABEL—amiable
MABILIA—lovable
MACRINA—docile
MADDIE—valued
MADELENA—very esteemed
MADELINE—esteemed
MADELLE—devout, loyal
MADGE—pearl
MADRA—maternal
MAE—bitterness
    (May)
MAGDALENE—revered
    (Maggie, Magda)
MAGNOLIA—lush, innocent
MAGPIE—mischievous
MAHARANI—princess
MAIDEN—sweet and fair
MAISIE—insouciant
MAI-TAI—exotic
MAJESTA—queenly
MAJESTIC—awe-inspiring
MALINA—talented, crafty
MAME—witty
MAMIE—flighty
MANDY—easygoing
MANETTE—spiteful
MANON—disagreeable

MANUELA—trustworthy
MARA—friendly, kind
MARALINE—even-tempered
MARCELLA—happy
   (Marcie)
MARCELLINA—wise
MARCIA—ravenous
MARELLA—grumpy
MARGARET—lustrous
MARGOT—precious
MARI—complaining
MARIA—rebellious
MARIAH—soft, gentle
MARIANNA—relentless
MARICE—spiteful
MARIE—feisty
MARIGOLD—golden flower
MARILYN—difficult, dour
MARINA—of the sea
MARIS—luminous
MARJORIE—rare
MARLA—insouciant
MARLENE—respected
MARNIE—friendly
MARTHA—radiant
MARTINA—bellicose
MARTINE—moody
MARY—rebellious
MATILDA—mighty
MATTIE—energetic
MAUDE—powerful
MAUREEN—dark, shrewd

MAURITA—gloomy
MAVERICK—independent
MAVIS—song thrush
MAXINE—supreme
MAY—rebellious
MAYDA—sweet maiden
MEDEA—ruler
MEGAN—sprite
(Meg)
MEHITABEL—happiness
(Hitty)
MELANIE—black
MELANTHA—subtle
MELBA—helper, friend
MELINDA—gentle
MELISSA—honeybun
MELITA—honeybee
MELLIE—complaisant
MELODY—tuneful, warbling
MELONIE—placid
MELVINA—tagalong
MEMORY—good learner
MERCEDES—rewarding, favoring
MERCY—merciful, gentle
MERIT—deserving
MERLE—chirping
MERRY—mirthful
MICHELLE—precious, special
MIDGE—little fly
MIDGET—petite
MIDNIGHT—gloomy, dark
MIGNON—dainty

MIKI—beloved
MILDRED—mild, skinny
MILLICENT—dauntless
    (Millie)
MILLISSA—pleasant
    (Lisa)
MILO—rhythmic
MIMI—resolute
MIMIC—imitative
MINA—well-trained
MINDFUL—good obeyer
MINDY—frisky
MINERVA—wise
MING—valuable, delicate
MING-POO—exotic, rare
MINNA—good memory, clever
    (Minnie)
MINX—tease, pert
MIRANDA—admired
MIRIAM—rebel
MISCHIEF—troubles, pranks
MISS—pert, rigorous
    (Missy)
MISTY—dreamy, sentimental
MITTENS—warmth
MITZY—single-minded
MODEST—humble, shy
MODESTA—chaste, sacred
MODESTY—decency, humbleness
MOIRA—arrogant
MOLASSES—light brown, sugar

MOLL—disobedient
  (Mollie, Molly)
MONA—loner
MONEY—priceless
  (Moneybags)
MONICA—cautious, wary
MONIQUE—exacting
MONKEY—acrobat, gymnast
  (Monkeyshines)
MOODY—gloomy
MOONSTONE—gemlike, lustrous
MOPEY—brooder, dawdler
MOPPET—baby, darling, cute
MOPSY—raggedy
MOUSE—timid, petite
MUFF—soft
  (Muffy)
MUFFIN—delectable
MUFFIT—affectionate
MURIEL—nymphlike, smart
MUTT—mongrel
MUZZY—cuddly
MYRA—wonderful
MYRNA—gentle, docile
MYRTLE—fragrant, sweet

Myrtle Doc Pokey Albert

N

NADA—hopeful
    (Nadine)
NAIDA—water nymph
NANCY—grace, mercy
    (Nan, Nanny, Nance)
NANETTE—grace, charm
NANON—dignity, charm
NAOMI—serene, even-tempered
NAPPY—sleepy, lazy
NARA—happy
NARCISSA—vain, arrogant, beauty
    (Narcissus)
NARCISSUS—flowerlike, cheerful
NARDA—sweet-smelling, clean
NATALIE—joyous, festive, happy
(Natalia, Nathalie, Natala, Natasha, Tash)
NATHANIA—delightful, enthusiastic
NATTY—trim, neat, tidy
NEBULA—misty eyed, opaque
NECESSITY—absolutely essential
NEDDA—protective
NELIA—strong
NELL—genial, clever
    (Nellie)
NELLWYN—convivial
NELMA—intelligent
NESTA—idolized, chaste

NETTA—polite, subtle
NETTIE—neat, fastidious
NIBBLER—skinny, picky
NICHOLE—harmonious
    (Nicolette)
NIKI—lovable
NINA—graceful
    (Ninette)
NINNY—slow mover
NITA—omnivorous
NOELLE—joyful, happy
NOLA—noble, famous
NONSENSE—silly, jovial
NORA—honorable
    (Norine)
NO-SHOW—forgetful, tardy
NUMSKULL—dunce
NYMPH—beautiful maiden

O

OBELIA—rich in warmth, love
OBLIGE—pleases, obeys
OCTAVIA—eighth born
ODDITY—different, particular
ODELIA—highly prized
ODETTE—impressive
OLGA—very blessed
OLIVE—lustrous skin, fruitful
    (Olivia, Ollie)
OLYMPIA—lofty, arrogant
OMEGA—last, the end
ONA—one and only
ONYX—black as night
OPAL—colorful, shiny
OPHELIA—siren
ORCHID—showy, proud
    (Orcus)
ORINA—golden-haired
ORLENA—flecked with gold

P

PADDYCAKE—scrumptilitious
PALMEDA—inventive
PALMIRA—achiever
PAMELA—honey and sweetness
    (Pam)
PAMONA—meek
PAMPER—gratify, indulge
PANDA—cuddly
PANDORA—mischievous
PANSY—pensive
PARFAIT—perfection
PASSION FLOWER—heart's delight
PATIENCE—steadfast, forebearing
PATRICIA—noble, patrician
    (Patsy, Patty, Pat, Tricia)
PAULETTE—small, petite
    (Pauline)
PEABODY—busybee
PEACEFUL—calm, serene
PEACHES—genial, gay
PEARL—having luster, glowing
PEBBLES—spotted
PECAN—nutlike, minute
PEEK-A-BOO—evasive, sly
PEEWEE—cute
PEGASUS—winged horse
PEGGY—lustrous, shiny

PENELOPE—inventive, subtle
  (Pen, Penny)
PEONY—blossoming
PEPITA—prolific
PERA—cocky, arrogant
PERDITA—lost, wandering
PERFECTA—faultless
PERKY—self-assured
PERSIA—silky, smooth
PERSIS—two-faced
PETRINA—dependable
PETRONELLA—reliable
PETUNIA—perky, omnivorous
PHEODORA—the adored
PHERES—keen, perceptive
PHILBERTA—brilliant
PHILIPPA—lover of horses
  (Philly, Phyllis, Phil)
PHILOMENA—benevolent
PHOEBE—smart, shrewd
PHOENIX—bird, zenith
PIGEON—bird, stout
PING-PONG—never decisive
PINK LADY—feminine
PINKY—delicate
PINON—restraining
PIPER—lithe
PIPPA—saucy
PIXIE—elfin
PLACIDIA—serene
PLEASANT—good-natured
PLEASURE—joy, delight

Petunia

PLUM—delectable
POLLY—rebel
   (Pollyana)
POOJIE—rascal
POPPET—lovable
POPPY—wild, colorful
PORTIA—piggly-wiggly
POSY—happy face
POTTS—tubby
PRIDE—dignity, vanity
PRIMA—first
PRIMPER—vain, self-satisfied
PRIMROSE—genial, gay
   (Rose)
PRINCESS—royal
PRISCILLA—traditional, prescriptive
   (Pris, Prissy)
PRUDENCE—discreet, prudent,
   circumspect (Pru)
PRUNELLA—wrinkled, spiteful
PSYCHE—soulful
PUFF—elated, excited
PUG—squat, wrinkled
PUMPKIN—rotund
PUNKY—dour-faced
PURITY—chastity

Q

QUEEN—regal
    (Queenie)
QUINTINA—the fifth

R

RACHEL—lamb, gentle
RADIANT—shining
RAGGEDY—shaggy
RAINA—duchess
RAMAH—leader
RAMONA—wise, protector
RANA—imperial
RANDOM—haphazard
RAPHAELA—healer
RAPUNZEL—long-haired
RAVEN—ensnare, trap
RAVENA—sombre
REA—lanky, lithe
REBATE—return, extra
REBECCA—trap, snare
   (Becky, Reba)
REGINA—queen
RENA—nymphlike
RENATA—reborn
RENE—self-poised
RENÉE—fresh, clean, reborn
RETA—sophisticated
RHAPSODY—improviser
RHEA—"mother of the gods"
RHODA—a rose
RITA—rare, special

RITZ—the best
    (Ritzy)
RIVA—dreamer
ROANNA—easygoing
ROBERTA—well-liked, intelligent
    (Robin, Robina, Robyn, Robbie)
RODERICA—leader, liked
ROLANDA—earth-lover
ROSA—rose
ROSAMOND—fair rose
ROSANNA—graceful
ROSE—beautiful flower
    (Rosabelle, Rosalie, Rosaline, Rosanne)
ROSEBUD—precious
ROSEMARY—sweet, fragrant
    (Rosemarie)
ROSETTA—little rose
ROSINA—optimistic
ROSY—blushing
ROUDY—spunky, active
ROWENA—coercive
ROXANNE—dewy-eyed
    (Rosana, Roxy)
RUBY—reddish, gemlike
RUE—sorrowful
RUFFLES—frilly
RUMBA—smoothly undulating
RUSTY—awkward
RUTH—beauty

S

SABA—healthy, energetic
SABRINA—faithful
SACHA—considerate
SADIE—princess
SALINA—salty, briny
SALLY—noble
SALOME—peaceful
SALTY—weathered, pungent
SAMARA—guardian
SAMELLA—loving
SANDRA—friend, helper
    (Sandy)
SAPPHIRE—blue-eyed
SARAH—princess
    (Sadie, Sally, Sara, Sarita)
SASHA—cute, petite
SASSAFRAS—spicy, fragrant
SASSY—saucy
SATIN—smooth, glossy
SAUCY—pert, coercive
SCAMP—playful, rambunctious
SCARLET—fiery
SCHEHERAZADE—queenly
    (Scher, Zadie)
SCRATCHES—claws, digs
SCRUPLES—qualms
SEBASTIONA—venerable

SECUNDA—the second
SELENA—moonstruck
SELMA—volatile
SEPTIMA—seventh child
SERAFINA—ardent, loving
SERENA—tranquil, serene
SHADOW—reflection
SHADY—tricky, clever
SHAGGY—coarse, tangled, matted
SHALIMAR—exotic
SHALOM—peace, hello, goodbye
SHAMMY—soft
SHANI—pale colored
    (Shanna)
SHANNON—quick-tempered
SHARON—moody
SHAWN—feisty
SHEBA—feline
SHEILA—blind
SHELLY—sealike
SHERBET—frosty
SHERRY—wine colored
SHIRLEY—peaceful, chaste
SHOO SHOO—busybody
SHORTY—stubby, undersize
SHY—timid
SIBONE—know-it-all
    (Sibyl)
SIDONIE—enchantress
SILKY—slinky, smooth
SILVER—costly, gray
SILVIA—tree climber

SIREN—temptress
SISSY—prissy, cowardly
SISTER—familial
SIZZLE—quick temper
SLEEPY—lazy, lethargic
SLINKY—slithery
SMUDGE—messy, blurry
SNOOKS—good disposition
SNOOP—sneaky, inquisitive
SNOOZER—sleepy
SNOWBALL—frosty white, clean
SOAPY—fluffy, bubbly
SOFTNESS—furry, comfy
SONIA—wise
SOPHIA—crafty
   (Sophy)
SPANKY—brisk
SPARKLE—vivacious, lively
SPARROW—bird, little
SPEED—swift
   (Speedy)
SPHINX—poker faced, enigmatic
SPICE—lively, zestful
SPOOKIE—scared, frightening
SPOT—haphazard, random
   (Spots, Spotty)
SPRITE—ghostlike, elfin
SQUEEKY—noisy
STACY—quiet, calm
STAR—attention getter
STELLA—performer
STEPHANIE—crowned

STERLING—true blue, trust
STOCKINGS—distinctive marks
STORMY—fiery, feisty
STREAK—swiftness
STYLE—demeanor
SUDS—frothy, bubbly
SUE—slender lily
SUGAR—sweet
SUKEY—fast runner
SUNDAE—delicious
SUNFLOWER—favorite
SUNNY—optimistic
SUNSHINE—lovely to behold
SUSAN—fragility
    (Susanne, Suzette, Suzy)
SUZY-Q—charmer
SWEETIE—lover, affectionate
SWEET PEA—slender
SWIFT—fast

T

TABASCO—saucy, tart
TABITHA—gazelle
   (Tabby)
TACITA—silent, docile
TAFFY—light-colored
TALITHA—maiden, innocent
TALLULAH—actress
   (Tally, Talia, Lu, Lulu, Lalie)
TAMA—gentle movements
TAMARA—stately, regal
   (Tammy, Tam)
TANGO—slinky
TANIA—nordic, arrogant
TARA—earthly
TASHA—imperial
TEENY—tiny
TEMPERANCE—moderation
TERESA—omnivorous
TERRY—pretty eyes
TESS—provider, gatherer
   (Tessa, Tessie)
THADDEA—worthy of praise
THALIA—new, lively
THANKFUL—special, grateful
THEA—supreme
THEDA—divine
THEKLA—renown

THELMA—nursling
THEODORA—loving
 (Theo, Dorie)
THERESA—saintly
THOMASA—imitative
 (Thomasina)
THUMPER—nervous
TIBBY—fluttery
TIDBIT—little thing
TIFFANY—exacting
 (Tiffy)
TIGER—aggressive
TIKO—bouncy
TILDA—mighty, strong
 (Tilly)
TIMOTHEA—honorable
TINA—lithe
TINKA—clever, shrewd
TINKERBELLE—artful
TINY—little, petite, elfin
TISH—bright, sharp
TOADIE—irascible
TOBA—goodness
TODY—wide-eyed
TOINETTE—romanesque, statuesque
TOKEN—remembrance
TOLLY—alluring
TOOTS—carefree
 (Tootsie)
TOPAZ—precious
TOPSY—turnabout
TOPY—light-headed

TOURMALINE—rare
TRACY—imitative
TRICIA—patrician
TRINKET—trifle
TRIVEA—paltry, insignificant
TRIXIE—pixie, gnomelike
TROUBLES—problems, misfortunes
TROY—stoic
TRUDY—big-eyed
    (Trude, Truffles)
TRUE—loyal
TUBBY—rotund
TUDIE—content
TULIP—fresh, well-formed
TURQUOISE—pale green-eyed
TURTLE DOVE—sweet thing
TUTU—very short
TWEETIE—chirping
    (Tweetie-Bird)
TWIGGY—lanky, stylish
TWINKLE—scintillate
    (Twinky)

U

UDELE—prosperous
ULA—jewel of the sea
ULRICA—ruler, leader
UNA—the one
UNDINE—wavy, flowing, curly
URSA—fearless, dauntless
    (Ursula, Ursel)

V

VAGUE—confused, sleepy
VALENCIA—strong
VALENTINE—valorous, healthy
    (Tina, Valentina)
VALERIE—rigorous, brave
    (Val, Valoria)
VANESSA—butterfly
VANIA—spiritual
VARINA—stranger
VASHTI—beautiful
VEDA—knowledgeable, smart
VELDA—wise, awesome
VELMA—protector
VELVET—soft
VENETIA—good-natured
VENUS—love and beauty
VERA—truth
VERBENA—fragrant flower
VERDA—fresh
VERENA—wise
VERNA—new, springlike
VERONICA—true image
    (Vera, Ronny)
VESTA—goddess of virgins
VICTORY—victorious, winner
    (Victoire, Vicky, Victoria)
VIDA—beloved

VIM—energetic, determined
VINCENTIA—conquerer
VINEY—clinging
VINNEY—mellow
VIOLA—elusive, fragile
    (Violet)
VIRGINIA—springlike, zesty
VIRGO—dutiful
VIVIAN—animated
VOLETTA—mysterious

W

WANDA—wanderer, roamer
WANNETTA—pale one, clean
WELCOME—convivial, friendly
WENDELIN—stray, meander
    (Wendy)
WHIM—caprice, fancy
WHIZZ—smart, swift
WIGGER—jiggler, totter
WIGGLES—shake, rattle and roll
WILHELMINA—resolute, dependable
WILLABELLE—willowy, lithe
    (Willa)
WILLETTA—weeping, sad
    (Willie)
WILLOW—praiseworthy
WINDY—stormy, breezy
WINIFRED—peaceful
    (Winnie, Freddie)
WINKEY—bright-eyed
WINONA—firstborn daughter
WISHES—hopes and dreams
WITCH—bewitching, enchanting
WYNNE—innocent, clean

X

XANTHE—yellow-haired
XENIA—hospitable, genial
XIMENA—insouciant

Y

YOLANDA—meritorious
YSOLDE—fair, chaste
YVETTE—fearless, impulsive
YVONNE—rigorous, commendable

Lady, Robin, Polly

Z

ZADY—princess
ZANDRA—helpful, dutiful
ZARA—zany, gay
ZELDA—staunch, immovable
ZENA—feminine
ZENIA—generous, kind
ZENOBIA—exemplary, exacting
ZEPHYR—gentle, breezy
ZETA—the sixth
ZINNEA—showy, coercive
ZIPPER—brisky, snappy
ZITA—determined, severe
ZOE—life
ZSA ZSA—pretty, gay, zesty
ZULEIKA—unblemished, comely

MALE NAMES

A

AARON—lofty
ABEL—vain
ABNAKI—sun worshiper
ABNER—light
ABRAHAM—father of multitudes
    (Abe, Abie)
ACE—quality, unity
ACHILLES—hero
ADAM—manly
ADOLPH—noble
    (Dolph)
ADONIS—lord, youthful
ADRIAN—black
AESOP—fable
AGATE—gem
AJAX—eagle
ALADDIN—heroic
ALAN—harmony
    (Al)
ALBERT—noble, bright
    (Al, Bert)
ALDEN—protector
ALEXANDER—aid, helpful
    (Alec, Alex, Sandy)
ALEXIS—promoter, helpful
ALFIE—loyal

ALFONSE—determined, eager
(Alfonso, Fonsie)
ALFRED—psychic
(Al, Alf, Alfie)
ALGERNON—bewhiskered, whiskers
(Algy)
ALI—friend
ALLISTER—assist
ALONZO—warrior
(Lon)
ALOYSIUS—famous
ALPHA—first, bright
ALVIN—beloved
AMBER—golden
AMBROSE—immortal
(Nam)
AMIGO—friend
AMOS—burden-bearer
ANASAZI—ancient
ANDREW—manly
(Andy)
ANGEL—messenger
ANGUS—strong
ANTHONY—inestimable, valuable
(Tony)
ANTON—unbelievable
APACHE—the enemy
APOLLO—wizard
AQUARIUS—water carrier
ARCHIBALD—prince
(Archie, Archy, Baldie)
ARGUS—vigilant

ARIES—the ram
ARIKANA—corn-eater
ARISTOTLE—philosopher
ARNOLD—strong
   (Arnie)
ARROW—pointer, straight-forward
ARTEMUS—brave, courageous
   (Artie)
ARTHUR—valorous, noble
   (Art, Artie)
ASA—healthy
ASHER—cheerful, happy
ASHLEY—staunch
   (Ash)
ASMUS—beloved
ASPEN—gangly
ATAKAPA—man-eater
ATLAS—strong
AUBREY—authoritative
AUGUST—dignified
AUGUSTUS—majestic
   (Gus)
AUSTIN—exalted
AVERY—farseeing, assertive
AXEL—grateful
AZAZEL—evil spirit
AZTEC—tawny

B

BAGGY—droopy
BAMBI—doe, baby deer, soft
BANDIT—desperado
BANJO—plucky
BANNER—commander
BAPTISTE—Christian
BARDO—digger
BARLOW—dweller
BARNABAS—prophet
   (Barnaby, Barney)
BARNETT—commander
BARNEY—swift
BARRETT—strong
BARRON—noble warrior
BARRY—marksman
BARTH—sheltering
BARTHOLOMEW—earthy
   (Bart, Bat, Batty, Bartley)
BASIL—kingly
BATTY—funny
BAXTER—baker
BEASTIE—active
BEAU—lover, dandy
BEAUREGARD—soldier
BECKET—saint
BEE-BEE—accurate
BENEDICT—blessed

BENJAMIN—loyal
  (Ben, Benny, Benjie)
BENTLEY—classy
BERNARD—bearlike, black
  (Bernie, Barney)
BERT—bright
BERTRAM—bright raven
BETA—second
BIFF—jovial
BIG-BOY—giant
BIJOU—crystal clear
BINGO—gambler
BINKY—good-natured
BITSEY—little one
BITTY—small, tiny
BLABBERMOUTH—talkative
BLACKIE—dark one
BLAINE—thin, lean
BLAIR—quiet, simple
BLAKE—black
BLITZ—raid
BLITZEN—speedy, dynamic
BLOCKHEAD—vague
BLUE—melancholy
BO—lover
BOFFO—variety
BOJO—musical
BON-BON—good, bonus
BONG—rhythmical
  (Bongo)
BLAZE—fiery
BONITO—handsome

BOO—frightening
BOO-BOO—disapproving
BORIS—warrior
BOSCO—saint
BOURBON—relaxing, mellow
BOWIE—knife, sharp
BOWSER—archer, accurate
BOYD—yellow-haired
BOZO—clumsy
BRADFORD—openhearted, liberal
    (Bradley, Brad)
BRADLEY—lean
    (Brad)
BRADY—repetitious
BRANDON—energetic, commanding
BRANT—agitator
BREEZY—windy
BRENT—trustworthy
BRETT—staunch, sturdy
    (Bret)
BREWSTER—thirsty
BRIAN—strong
    (Bryan)
BRIGHT—lively
BRINDLE—dark streaks
BRIT—ruddy
BRITCHES—spotted
BROWNIE—cheerful goblin
BRUCE—devious
BRUNO—dark-complexioned
BRUT—ruthless
BRUTUS—unreasonable

BRYCE—speedy, quick
BUB—friend
BUBA—bubble
BUCK—strong
BUDDY—friend
BUG-A-BOO—mistake
BUGGY—creeping, crawling
BUGSY—small creature
BULLET—fast
BUMBLEBEE—bright color, buzzy
BUNKY—nonsense
BUNNY—fluffy, soft
BUNZY—nestling
BURTON—glorious raven
    (Berton, Bert, Burt)
BUSTER—close friend
BUTCHIE—bristly
BUTTERSCOTCH—flavorful, golden
BUZZ—hum
    (Buzzy)
BUZZY—humming, flighty
BYRON—homey

C

CADET—well-behaved
CADWALLER—orderly, neat
CAESAR—hairy
CALEB—trustworthy
    (Cal)
CALVERT—herdsman, herder
    (Cal)
CALVIN—bald
    (Cal)
CALYPSO—musical
CANNON—swift, noisy
CANUTE—king
    (Nute)
CAPRICORN—celestial
    (Cappy, Corny)
CAPTAIN—commander
    (Cappy)
CARL—manly
    (Carlo, Carlos)
CARLETON—hard-driver
CARLISLE—inscrutable, mysterious
    (Carlyle)
CARMICHAEL—immortal
CARROLL—fallible
CARTER—digger
CASEY—valorous
CASH—wealthy

CASIMIR—peaceful
(Kasmir)
CASPAR—treasure, rich
(Casper)
CASS—vain
CASSIDY—ingenious
CASTOR—industrious beaver
CATO—cautious
CECIL—blind
CEDAR—fragrant
CEDRIC—chieftain
CEPHAS—rocklike, sturdy
CHAD—considerate
CHAMOIS—soft, buff
(Shammy)
CHAMPAGNE—sparkle, bubbly
CHAMPION—defender
CHANCELLOR—disciplined
CHANGEABLE—moody
CHANOOK—agile
CHARCOAL—black, warm
CHARGER—commander, leader
CHARLES—manly
(Charlie, Charley, Chuck)
CHARMER—clever
CHARRO—black
CHAUNCEY—well-behaved
CHAUVINIST—self-satisfied
CHECKERS—colorful
CHEEKO—impudent
CHEMEHUEVI—swift of foot
CHENEY—peaceful

Anastasia & Charles

CHEROKEE—sturdy, mountaineer
CHESTER—diplomat
(Ches, Chet)
CHESTNUT—jokester
CHEYENNE—farmer
CHI—shy
CHICKASAW—fierce, independent
CHICO—peppy
CHIEF—leader
CHILLY—shivering, trembling
CHIP—token
CHIPPER—sprightly
CHIPPEWA—immense
CHIQUITO—boy
CHOCTAW—long hair
CHOPPER—hungry
CHORES—labor
CHOU—friendly
CHOWANOC—trustworthy
CHRISTOPHER—honorable
(Chris, Kit)
CHUBBY—plump
CHUM—friend
CHUMLEY—affectionate
CHUNKY—stocky
CICERO—philosopher
CID—hero
CINBAD—sailor, water-lover
CINDER—ashes
CINNAMON—reddish-brown
CIRO—independent
CISCO—daredevil

CLAIR—bright
CLANCY—Irish
CLARENCE—illustrious
    (Clare)
CLARET—reddish color
CLARK—loyal
    (Clarke)
CLAUDE—lame
    (Claudius, Claus)
CLAYTON—pliable
    (Clay)
CLEMENT—merciful
    (Clem)
CLIFFORD—secretive
    (Clifton, Cliff)
CLINTON—pleasant
    (Clint)
CLOUDY—gloomy
CLOVIS—spicy
CLYDE—loud
COCHISE—chief
COCO—husky
COCOA—soft brown
COCONINO—nutty
CODY—strong
COFFEE—zesty
COGNAC—bittersweet
COLBY—worker
COLONEL—leader
COMANCHE—conqueror
COMET—swift

COMMANDER—leader
CONCHO—shell
CONRAD—tactful
CONROY—wise
CONSTANTINE—forthright
    (Connie)
COPPER—reddish-gold
CORBET—a raven
    (Corbin, Corby)
CORDELL—a cord
CORKY—pluggy
CORNELIUS—hornlike, corny
CORT—loud mouth
CORTEZ—bold
CORWIN—devoted
CORY—regal
COTTON—soft, fluffy
CRABBY—ill-natured
CRAIG—rugged
CREEPER—crawler
CREEPY—shivery
CRICKET—chirping
CRISPIN—curly-haired
CRITTER—creature
CRUISER—traveler
CRUSOE—loner
CUB—cuddly
    (Cubby)
CUDDLES—snuggler
CULVER—a dove
CURLY—ringlet, natural

CURRAN—hero
CURTIS—well-behaved
    (Curt)
CYCLONE—whirlwind
CYCLOPS—farseeing
CYRANO—lovable
CYRIL—lordly
    (Cyrus, Cy)
CZAR—commander

D

DAFFY—foolish
DAGWOOD—forgetful
DALE—meander
DALTON—dedicated
DAMON—tame
    (Damian)
DAN—decisive
DANA—masterful
    (Dane, Dayn)
DANCER—quick mover, graceful
DANDY—first-rate
DANIEL—heroic
    (Dan, Danny)
DAPPER—alert, lively
DARAH—bold
DARBY—playful
DARCY—protective
DARK-EYES—soulful
DARYL—beloved
    (Darrell)
DAVID—beloved
    (Dave, Davy)
DEAN—wanderer
    (Deane)
DECEMBER—cheerful
DEE-DEE—soulful
DEMETRIUS—mighty

DEMON—evil spirit
DENNIS—god of wine, mellow
    (Denys)
DERRICK—leader, mighty
DESTINY—fate
DEVIL—wicked
DEWEY—cool
DEXTER—right-handed
DIABLO—tall, stately
DIAMOND—brilliant gem
DIEGO—stately, superior
DIGGER—delver, excavator
DIMITRI—godly
DIMWIT—obscure, vague
DING-A-LING—small, insignificant, dummy
DINGBAT—shabby, erratic
DINGY—absentminded
DINKY—small, tiny
DINO—luminescent
DION—warrior
DIRK—strong, quick
DIXON—swift
DIZZY—giddy
DOBIE—quiet
DOC—skillful, clever
    (Docky)
DOLITTLE—procrastinate
DOMINGO—authoratative
DOMINIC—Sunday's child
DOMINO—playful
DONALD—dark or brown, mighty
    (Don, Donny)

DONNER—swift
DOODLE—dawdle
DOODLEBUG—scratches
DORIAN—soldier, military
DOUGLAS—dark gray
  (Doug)
DOYLE—reserved
DREAMER—imaginative
DROOPY—sagging
DUCKY—quick
DUDLEY—distinguished
DUFFER—clumsy
  (Duffy, Duff)
DUKE—nobleman
DUMBO—simpleton
DUM-DUM—weakling
DUMPLING—eyeful
DUNCAN—warrior
  (Dunc)
DUNSTAN—rocklike, strong
DUSKY—twilight
DUSTY—powdery
DUTCH—troublesome
DWIGHT—white, fair
DYNAMITE—energetic

E

EAGLE—strong, graceful
EARL—intelligent
    (Earle)
EBEN—fortitude
    (Eb)
EBENEZER—helpful
EBONY—black
ECHO—repeat
EDAN—fire
EDBERT—prosperous, bright
EDGAR—piercing, sharp
EDMUND—protector
    (Edmond)
EDRED—helper
EDRIC—prosperous ruler
EDSEL—wealthy
EDSON—protective
EDWALD—powerful
EDWARD—guardian
    (Ed, Eddie, Ward)
EDWIN—friendly
EGAN—ardent
EGBERT—intelligent
EGERTON—homebody
EGMONT—powerful protector
ELBERT—noble, bright
ELDON—elflike

ELDRED—wise
   (Eldrid)
ELDWIN—small
ELF—mischievous
ELI—the highest
ELIAS—the highest
   (Eli)
ELIJAH—prophet
ELIOT—aid
   (Elliott)
ELISHA—exalted
ELLERY—outdoorsman
ELLIOT—to rescue, aid
ELLIS—unselfish, kind
ELMER—awesome
   (Elmar)
ELMO—amiable
ELROY—regal
ELSON—important
   (Elsen)
ELSU—falcon
ELTON—homebody
ELVIN—gnome
ELY—greatness
EMERY—industrious
   (Emory)
EMIL—clever
EMMANUEL—godly
   (Emanuel)
EMMET—industrious
   (Emmett)
ENOCH—teacher

Erasmus

ENOS—intense
ENRICO—front-runner
EPHRIM—dual
ERASMUS—beloved
ERASTUS—loved, amiable
    (Rastus)
ERIC—kingly
    (Erik, Erick)
ERIE—cat people
ERNEST—grave, serious
    (Ernst, Ernie)
ERROL—wanderer
ERWIN—friend in need
ESMOND—protective
ETHAN—strong
ETHELBERT—noble, bright
EUGENE—well-born
    (Gene)
EUSTACE—steadfast
    (Eustis)
EVAN—young warrior
EVERETT—strong, brave
    (Everitt, Everet)
EWALD—powerful
    (Evald)
EWART—wild boar
EXODUS—roamer
EZEKIEL—reverent
    (Zeke)
EZRA—helpful
    (Ez)

Felix, Snowy, Max

F

FABIAN—earthy
FALCON—hawk
FANCY—imaginative
FANG—sharp-toothed
FARLEY—superior
FARQUHAR—manly
FARREL—valorous
    (Farrell)
FATT-CAT—rotund
FEARLESS—brave
FEBRUARY—honorable
FELIPE—horse-lover
FELIX—happy, fortunate
FEODOR—gifted
FERDINAND—adventurous
    (Fernando)
FERGUS—manly, strong
FESTUS—gladiator
FIBBER—imaginative, talkative
FIDDLE—musical
FIDO—hound
FINIAN—colorful
FLAGG—reedy
FLASH—lightning
FLAVIAN—bright yellow
    (Flavius)
FLECK—spotted

FLICKA—quickly, gusty
FLICKER—streak, dash
FLIP—talkative
FLIPPER—saucy
FLOYD—gray
FLUBBER—bloated
FLUFFY—fatuous, silly
FOGGY—confused
FOLLY—ridiculous
FORREST—dense
   (Woody)
FORTIS—strong, gallant
FOSTER—adopted
FOXY—clever, crafty
FRAIDY—timid
FRANCHOT—freedom
   (Francis, Frank)
FRANCO—gregarious
FRANCOIS—friendly
FRANKLIN—independent
FRANZ—generous
FRECKLES—spotted
FREDERICK—peaceful, ruler
   (Frederic, Fred)
FREEDOM—independence
FRIAR—brotherly
FRIDAY—lovable
FRIENDLY—affectionate, comforting
FRISBEE—whirly
FRISKY—lively
FRITZ—peaceful ruler

FROSTIE—icy, cold
   (Frosty)
FROTHY—airy
FUNNY—amusing, comic
FURRY—shaggy
FUZZY—indistinct

G

GABBY—talkative
(Gaby)
GABRIEL—archangel
(Gabe, Gibbie)
GADABOUT—charmer
GADGET—small
GAGE—defiant
GAIL—lively
(Gale)
GANDER—goose
GARABALDI—patriot
GARCIA—warrior
GARDINER—guardian
GARGOYLE—grotesque
GARLAND—victorious
(Gar)
GARMON—warrior
GARNER—protective
(Gar)
GARRETT—soldier
(Garry, Gary)
GARRICK—warrior
GARTH—peaceful
GASPER—emotional
GASTON—steadfast
GEM—jewel
GENERAL—chief

GENIE—eerie, supernatural
GENIUS—brilliant
GEOFFREY—peaceful
GEORGE—nature-lover
GERALD—vigorous
    (Gerry, Garcia, Gerard)
GHANDI—leader
GHOST—spirit
GIANT—immense
GIDDY—dizzy
GIDEON—lumberjack
GIFFORD—brave
GIGGLES—laughing
GIGOLO—dancer
GILA—monster
GILBERT—faithful
    (Gilburt, Gelbert, Gil)
GILFORD—attentive
GILROY—knight
    (Gil, Roy)
GIMPY—lame
GINGER—spicy
GIUSEPPE—woodcarver
    (Pepe)
GIZMO—devising
GLEN—recluse
    (Glenn)
GLORY—magnificent
GODFREY—peaceful
GOGO—fast, quick
GOLD—yellow-colored
GOLDEN—brilliant yellow

GOOFY—silly
GOONEY—humorous
GORDO—plump
GORDON—thoughtful
    (Gordo, Gordie)
GORMAN—fearless
GRANT—great, large
GRAY—cheerless
GREGORY—watchful
    (Greg)
GRIFFITH—ruddy
    (Griff)
GRIT—unyielding
GRITS—corny
GRITTY—courageous
GRIZZLY—grayish
GROUCH—irritable
GROVER—farmer, earthy
GRUBBY—untidy
GRUMBLES—rumble
GRUMPY—surly
GUARDIAN—custodian
GUIDO—sensible
GUNNER—hunter
GUNTHER—kingly
GUSTAV—knave
    (Gustave, Gus)
GUY—lively
GYPSY—wanderer, traveler

H

HAAKON—clansman
HADWIN—warrior
HALBERT—bright stone
    (Hal)
HAMBONE—imitator
HAMISH—actor
HAMLET—prince
HAMLIN—hardy
    (Hamilyn)
HANS—everlasting
HANSEL—fortunate
HAPPY—cheerful, pleasant
HARDEN—swift, timid
HARLAN—leader
    (Harland)
HARLEY—virile, strong
HARMONY—calm
HAROLD—powerful warrior
    (Hal)
HARPO—plucky
HARRISON—shrewd
HARRY—superior
    (Hal)
HARTLEY—royal
    (Hart)
HARVEY—genial
HAVOC—confused

HAWK—bird of prey
HAZE—vague
HECTOR—defender
HEISHI—spirit
HENRY—manly
    (Hank, Hal)
HERBERT—warrior
    (Herb, Herbie)
HERMAN—soldier
    (Hermon)
HERO—strong
HICKORY—nutty
HIDATSA—seaworthy
HILARY—cheerful
    (Hillary, Hillery)
HIRAM—noble
    (Hy)
HIROSHI—generous
    (Hiro)
HOAGY—musical
HOBART—brilliant mind
HOBO—wanderer
HOCUS-POCUS—magical
HODGE-PODGE—helter-skelter
HOHOKAM—disappear
HOKAN—tribe
HOLDEN—kindly, gracious
HOMER—confident
HONEY—superlative
HONEYCOMB—checked
HOPI—peaceful
HOPPY—springy

HORACE—resolute
HORNET—buzzy
HOSEA—salvation
HOUDI—mystical
HOUDINI—magical
HOWARD—knight
    (Howie)
HOYT—mirthful
HUBERT—intelligent
HUFFY—angry
HUGH—spirit
    (Hugo, Huey, Hughie)
HUGHES—forceful
HUMBUG—nonsense
HUMPHREY—peaceful
    (Humfrey)
HUNTER—seeker
HURRICANE—cyclone

I

IAGO—stately
IAN—devout, dedicated
ICHABOD—humble
IGNATIUS—fiery
    (Ignace)
IGOR—lively
IKE—vigorous
ILBERT—cheerful
    (Bert)
INKY—black
    (Inkspot)
IRA—descendant
IROQUOIS—roamers
IRVING—water-lover
    (Irvin, Irwin, Irv)
ISAAC—joyful
    (Izaak, Ike)
ISAIAH—prophet
ISIDOR—moon god
    (Isadore, Izzy)
IVAN—kingly
IVANHOE—knight, strong
IVAR—archer
    (Iver, Ivor, Ivon, Iva)

J

JABEZ—sorrowful
JACK—spirit
   (Jay)
JACOB—superior
   (Jake)
JAMES—stately, superior
   (Jamie, Jem, Jembo, Jim, Jimbo,
   Jimmy)
JANGLES—musical
JANUARY—stormy
JAQUES—supplanter
JARVIS—piercing
JASON—healer
JASPER—meritorious
JAWS—crushing
JAZZ—lively
JAZZY—splashy
JEB—thoughtful
JEEPERS—creepers
JEFFREY—peaceful
   (Jeff)
JEKYLL—changeable
JEMEZ—twin
JEREMIAH—exalted
JEREMY—exalted
JEROME—sacred
   (Jerry)

JESS—believing
JESSE—awesome
    (Jess)
JESTER—entertaining, comic
JET—forceful
JETHRO—superior
JIG—dancer
JIGGER—tricky
JIGGLE—jerky
JIGGS—lively
JINGLES—musical
JINX—unlucky
JOAB—magnificent
JOACHIM—supreme
JOCKO—competitive
JODY—careful
JOEL—dutiful
JOHN—spiritual
    (Jon, Jack, Jay, Jackie, Jocko, Johnnie,
    Johnny)
JONAH—dove
JONAS—dove
JONATHAN—free spirit
JORDAN—freethinker
JOSEPH—enrich
    (Josef, Joe, Joey)
JOSH—prankster, jokester
JOSHUA—powerful
    (Josh)
JOSIAH—healer
    (Josh)
JOVE—amazing

JUAN—devout
JUDAS—traitor
JUDE—saint
JUDGE—authoritative
JUDSON—critical
JULIUS—youthful
    (Julian, Jules, Jule)
JULY—fulfillment
JUMBO—immense, enormous
JUNIOR—youthful
JUPITER—mythical
JUSTIN—just, upright
    (Justus)

K

KACHINA—dancer
KANE—tribute
KANGA—jumpy
KANSA—proud
KAPPA—tenth
KARL—manly
KARMA—decisive
KASIMIR—Indian goat
KASMIR—peaceful
KASPAR—valuable
   (Kass)
KAYDET—military
KEANE—fair, just
KEITH—lumberjack, woodsman
KEMPER—ambitious
KENNARD—bold lover
KENNETH—handsome
   (Ken, Kensie)
KENRIC—ruler
KENTON—pallid
   (Kent)
KEPI—military cap
KERMIT—armor-clad
KERNEL—nutty
KERRY—swarthy
KERT—friendly
KESTER—clever

KEVIN—honorable
KIBITZ—adviser
KICKAPOO—unconquered
KILLER—fierce
KIM—chief
KING—top authority
KIOWA—proud
KIP—chief
KIRBY—dedicated
    (Kerby)
KISMET—fate
KIVA—small, sacred
KLAUS—bearded
KOKO—humorous
KONRAD—agent
KOOKY—fun-loving
KRINKLE—wrinkled

L

LAD—friend
LADDIE—youthful
   (Laddy)
LAFAYETTE—nobleman
LAIRD—proprietor
LAMBERT—bright
LANCELOT—knight
LANKY—awkward
LANNY—lean
LARS—victorious
   (Larz)
LAWRENCE—honorable
   (Laurence, Larry, Lorry, Lauren, Lars,
   Larz)
LAZARUS—humble
LAZY—sluggish
LAZYBONES—slow moving
LEANDER—courageous
LEAR—seaman
LEIGH—meadowlark
   (Lee)
LELAND—songbird
   (Lee)
LENNOX—chieftain
   (Lenox, Len)
LEO—lionhearted
LEON—lionlike

LEONARD—lionlike
LEOPOLD—prince
　(Lee)
LEROY—king
　(Roy)
LESLIE—friar
　(Les)
LESTER—legionnaire
LEVI—harmonious
LEWIS—warrior
　(Lew)
LIBERATOR—free
LIBRA—sacred, divine
LIEUTENANT—high official, military
LIGHTNING—flashing
LIMPET—shellfish
LINCOLN—chain
　(Link)
LINDO—ashen, blanched
LINK—bond
LINUS—small lion
LION—shaggy cat
LIONEL—little lion
LITTLE-ONE—smallest
LLOYD—gray
LOGY—lazy
LON—solitary
LORD—powerful, authoritative
LOREDO—learned
LOREN—victorious
　(Lorin, Lauren, Lorry)
LORENZO—laurel, honorable

LORING—commanding
LOTHARIO—famous warrior
LOUIS—hero
   (Luis, Lou, Louie)
LOWELL—beloved
LUCAS—luminous
LUCIFER—fallen angel
LUCIUS—light, bright
   (Lucian, Lucien, Luke)
LUCKY—fortunate
LUDLOW—prince
LUDWIG—soldier
LUKE—light, white
   (Lucas)
LUMPY—shapeless
LUTHER—warrior
LUXOR—comfort
LYNN—angry
   (Linn)

M

MAC—frugal
MACK—tremendous, ample
MADOC—beneficent
MAGICIAN—clairvoyant, sly
MAGINNIS—Scottish terrier
MAGNUS—great
MAHARAJA—prince
MAJESTY—splendor
MAJOR—great importance
MALARKEY—pretentious
MALCOLM—servant, saintly
   (Mal)
MALLORY—omen
MALVIN—servant
   (Melvin)
MANCHU—nomad
MANDAN—white chief
MANDEL—mantlerock
MANDRAKE—sorcerer
MANFRED—peaceful
MANLEY—virile, strong
   (Manly)
MANNY—devout
MANUEL—godly
   (Manny)
MANVILLE—wealthy
MARBLE—dark and light

MARCEL—curly
MARCELLUS—ruddy
   (Marcus)
MARCH—progressive
MARCO—inventive
MARCUS—possessive
   (Mark, Marc)
MARIO—bittersweet
MARION—acrid
MARLIN—sparrowhawk
   (Merlin)
MARLOWE—spearfish
   (Marlow)
MARMADUKE—sea leader
MARMION—sparkling
MARS—god of war
MARSHALL—high official
   (Marshal)
MARSTON—orderly
MARTIAL—warlike
MARTIN—war god
   (Marty, Tino)
MARVEL—wondrous
MARVIN—first-rate
   (Marwin, Marv)
MARX—shield
MASCOT—friendly
MASTER—authoritative
MATO—brave
MATTHEW—devout
   (Matt)

MAURICE—dark-skinned
   (Maury, Moris)
MAXIMILIAN—emperor
   (Max, Maxie)
MAXIMUS—inventor, inventive
MAXWELL—scientific
   (Max)
MAYNARD—mighty
MEATHEAD—inattentive, confused
MEDWIN—powerful friend
MELDON—millstone
MELLOW—mild
MELVILLE—servant
   (Mel)
MELVYN—chieftain
MERCURY—cunning, speed
MEREDITH—harmonious
   (Meridith)
MERLE—blackbird
MERRICK—deserving, worthy
MERRIT—worthy
   (Merritt)
MERTON—woodsman
   (Mert)
MERWIN—waterbug
   (Merwyn)
MESSENGER—forerunner
MEYER—steward
MICAH—prophet
MICHAEL—archangel
   (Mick, Mickey, Mike)

MIDAS—powerful
MIDGET—dwarf, very small
MIDNIGHT—swarthy, dark
MILES—soldier
    (Myles)
MILO—soldier
MILTON—millstone
    (Milt)
MING—artistic
MINT—fragrant, flavorful
MINUS—negative
MIRAGE—illusion
MISCHIEF—annoying, mischievous
MISTER—gentleman, sir
MITCHELL—devout, reverent
MITE—strong
MOBY—huge, immense
MOE—grim
MOGOLLON—mysterious
MOHAVE—inherent, intrinsic
MOLASSES—brownish
MONDAY—dreamy, moony
MONEY—wealthy
MONK—friar
MONROE—seaworthy
    (Monro, Munro)
MONTAGUE—artistic
    (Monty)
MOODY—gloomy
MOON—dreamer
MOONY—nonsense
MOOSE—large elk, antlered

MOP—absorbing
   (Moppy)
MORRIS—secure
   (Morice, Morry)
MORTIMER—sea warrior
   (Mort)
MORTON—earthy
MOSES—prophet, lawgiver, liberator
   (Mose)
MUFF—cluster of feathers
MUFFIN—crispy
MUGGINS—photogenic
   (Muggs)
MURDOCK—protective
MURRAY—cheerful
MUSCLES—strong, strength
MUTT—cur, mongrel
   (Muttzie)
MUZZY—fuzzy
MYRON—smokey

Mortimer, Marcie, Zeke

N

NAM—immortal
NAPOLEON—emperor
    (Nap, Nappy)
NAPPY—sleepy, drowsy
NARCISSUS—vain, arrogant, beauty
NATHAN—patriotic
    (Nat, Nate, Natty, Nattie)
NATTY—neat, tidy
NAVAJO—newcomer
NEAL—champion
    (Neil)
NEB—bird's beak
NEEDLES—gibe
NEHEMIAH—leader, comforter
NELSON—champion
    (Nels)
NEON—glowing
NEPTUNE—god of the sea
NESTOR—friendly, affectionate
NEVILLE—neighborly
    (Nev, Nevin)
NEWELL—kernel
NEWTON—amicable
NICHOLAS—triumphant
    (Nicolas, Nick, Nicky, Nicol)
NIFTY—proud
NIGEL—black

NINIAN—cloudy
NINNY—simpleton
NIPPER—sharp, biting
NIPPY—chilly
NOAH—patriarch
    (Noe)
NOBLE—illustrious
NOEL—musical
NOLAN—famous
    (Noland)
NOODLES—simple
NORBERT—bright
NORMAN—conqueror
NOVEMBER—eleventh
NOWELL—cheerful
NUBBY—rough-textured
NUTMEG—spicy
NUTTY—foolish
    (Nut, Nuttie)

O

OBADIAH—superb
OBERT—brilliant
OBIE—broad
   (Obé)
OCTAVIUS—eighth born
OGDEN—determined
   (Ogdon)
OLAF—saintly
OLEG—showy
OLIVER—saint, martyr
OLYMPUS—lofty
OMAR—entertaining
OMEGA—last, end
ORACLE—great authority
ORASTUS—argumentative
ORIN—white
   (Oran)
ORLANDO—famous
ORMAND—the bear
   (Ormond)
ORPHEUS—musical
ORSON—the bear
ORVILLE—glaring
   (Orval)
OSBORN—family man
OSCAR—bouncy
OSMUND—protective

OSWALD—powerful
OTHELLO—champion
OTIS—keen-hearing
OTTAWA—shrewd traders
OTTO—wealthy
OUIJA—mystical
OWEN—young warrior

P

PABLO—outstanding
PADDY—silent, quiet
PAL—friend
PALEY—small
PANCHO—wooly
PANDA—bear
PANTHER—fierce
PAPAGO—small people
PATCHES—multicolored
PATIENCE—calm
PATRICK—noble
   (Patric, Pat, Paddy)
PAUL—small
PAWS—clumsy
PAX—peaceful
PAYTON—noble
   (Peyton)
PEACEFUL—restful
PEANUT—herb, nutty
PEBBLES—crinkled
PECOS—large city
PEDRO—exhausted
PEEWEE—very small
PEPPER—spicy, black and white
PEPPY—energetic, fiery
PERCIVAL—companion, friend
   (Percy, Perce)

PERO—dog
PESO—dignified
PETER—rock, stony, strong
PHELAN—wolf
PHILANDER—humanitarian
PHILBERT—brilliant
PHILIP—horse-lover
    (Phil, Phip, Pip)
PHINEAS—oracle
PHOENIX—reborn, bird
PIED (PIPER)—leader
PIERRE—strong
PIMA—negative
PING—sharp
PINKY—little finger
PIP—small, speck
PIRO—homestead
PISCES—fish, water-lover
PIUS—holy
PLACID—easygoing, relaxed
PLATO—friendly
PLUNKET—harsh
PLUTO—wealthy
POCO—little
POGO—jumpy
POKEY—creepy
POMPEY—ancient
    (Pompeii)
POM-POM—rotund, fluffy
PONG—batty
POOCHIE—hound
POOH—scornful

POPEYE—bulgey
POWER—mighty
PRANCER—swagger
PRETZEL—ramify, diverge, puzzling
PRICKLY—stinging
PRIDE—proud
PRIMO—first rate
PRINCE—royalty
PROSPER—successful
PROTECTOR—guardian
PUDD—muddle
PUDGIE—chubby
PUFF—seabird
PUG—boxer
PUMPKIN—prickly
    (Punkin, Punkie, Punky)
PUNCHY—enervated
PYGMALION—sculptor, changeable

Q

QUACK—noisy
QUAPAW—water-lover
QUENTIN—fifth born
QUICK—speedy, rapid
QUIGLEY—loping
QUINCIE—fifth place
　　(Quincy)
QUINN—wise

R

RADAR—beaming, flashing
RADCLIFFE—red cliff, ruddy
RADFORD—solid
RAGS—stringy
RAJAH—Indian prince
RALPH—fierce, crafty
   (Rolph, Rafe)
RAMSEY—extreme, intense
   (Ramsay)
RANDOLPH—crafty, fierce
RANGER—soldier
RAPHAEL—angel
RASMUS—native
RASTUS—homebody, amiable
RATCHET—pivotal, meander, weave
RATTLES—clattering, shaky
RAVEN—black bird
RAYMOND—wise protector
   (Raymund)
RAYNARD—sage
   (Ray)
RAZZ—tantalize, irritate
REBEL—rebellious
RED—coppery
RED-FOX—clever, crafty
REDMOND—protective
   (Redmund, Red)

137

REGAN—kingly
REGGIE—powerful
REGINALD—powerful
    (Reg, Reggie)
REMUS—twin
REUBEN—distinguished
    (Rube)
REX—king
REXFORD—prince
RICHARD—strict
    (Dick, Dickie, Rick, Ritchie, Rich, Ricky)
RICKY—noble
RICO—skipping
RIPOFF—costly
RIP VAN WINKLE—sleepyhead
RISKIT—daring
RITZY—sociable
ROACH—silver-white fish
ROAMER—wanderer
ROBERT—famous
    (Bob, Bobbie, Bobby, Rob, Robby, Robbie)
ROBIN—bright
ROBINSON—musical
ROBOT—mechanical
ROBYN—bird
ROCHESTER—city slicker
ROCKY—swaying
RODERICK—famous ruler
    (Rod, Roddy)
RODNEY—servant
    (Rod, Roddy)
ROGER—sharp

ROLAND—famous
   (Rowland, Rollin, Rollo)
ROLLO—hunter
ROMAN—affectionate
ROMULUS—twin
RONALD—powerful
   (Ron, Ronnie, Roo)
ROOKIE—beginner
ROSCOE—ranger
ROSS—horse
ROSWELL—mighty steed
ROVER—wanderer
ROWDY—rough
ROYAL—regal
   (Roy, Royce)
RUDDY—reddish complexion
RUDOLPH—reddish
   (Rudy)
RUDYARD—slight, slender
RUFF—feathery
RUFFLES—feathered, trouble
RUFUS—red-haired
   (Rufe, Ruffie)
RULER—govern
RUNNER—rush
RUPERT—famous, bright
RUSSELL—red fox
RUSTY—sturdy
RUTHERFORD—cattleman, herder

Sam, Goldie, Nymph

S

SABER—sharp, piercing
SABIN—loyal
SAGE—grave, solemn
SAGITTARIUS—archer, accurate
SAKI—spicy
SALADO—rare
SALMON—anadromous fish
SALTY—earthy
SALVADORE—friendly
SAMBO—swarthy
SAMSON—robust
    (Sampson, Sam, Sammy)
SAMUEL—attentive
    (Sam, Sammy)
SANDER—promoter
    (Saunder, Sandy)
SANDOR—helpful
    (Sandro, Sandy)
SANDY—courageous
SANFORD—loyal
    (Sancho, Santos)
SASSY—saucy
SATCHMO—lovable
SATURDAY—seventh
SATURN—god of agriculture
SAUCY—smart
SAUL—decisive

141

SAWYER—lumberman
SAXON—swordsman
SCAMPER—playful, imp
SCAT—scoot
SCHNAPPES—nippy
SCHWATZIE—black
SCOOTER—quick
SCORPIO—eighth
SCOTT—Scotsman, practical
SCOUNDREL—villain, troublesome
SCOUT—watchful
SCRAPPER—quarrelsome
    (Scrappy)
SCROOGE—ill-natured, cantankerous
SCUFF—shuffle
    (Scuffy)
SCURRY—brisk
SEARLE—defender
    (Serle, Serlo)
SEBASTIAN—venerable
    (Sabby, Saba)
SEBERT—conqueror
SEBOLD—brave
SEDGWICK—victorious
    (Sedge)
SELBY—congenial
SEMAR—modest, shy
SENATOR—authoritative
SENIOR—elder
SEPTEMBER—ninth
SERGEANT—officer

SERGIO—romantic, lovable
    (Sergius)
SETH—agreeable, outstanding
SEWARD—guardian
SEXTUS—sixth
SEYMOUR—retiring
SHABBY—ill-kept
SHADOW—shady
SHADRAC—warrior
    (Shad)
SHADY—tranquil
SHAGGY—matted
    (Shag)
SHAH—king
SHAKEY—tremble
SHALIMAR—vague, artful
SHALOM—friendly
SHAMMY—soft
SHAMU—thrash, jumpy
SHAMUS—curious
SHANE—classy
SHANNON—stylish
SHAUGHNESSEY—trim, neat
SHAWN—grateful
SHAWNEE—wanderer
SHEIK—Arab chief
SHELBY—homebody, farmer
SHELLEY—creative
SHERMAN—shearer
SHERRY—mellow
SHERWIN—friendly

SHERWOOD—woodcutter
SHIFTY—tricky
SHOO—frighten
SHORTY—insufficient
SHOTSIE—accurate
SHUDDER—shiver
SHU-SHU—quickly
SHY—timid, bashful
SIBLEY—prophetic
SIDNEY—mellow, mellifluous
    (Sydney, Sid)
SIEGFRIED—peaceful
    (Sigfrid)
SIGH—yearn, grieve
SIGMUND—protector
SIGWALD—powerful
SILAS—fearless
SILKY—smooth
SILVANOS—forest-loving
    (Silvano)
SILVER—bright
SILVESTER—nature-loving
    (Sylvester, Silvio)
SIMBA—leader
SIMON—good listener
    (Simeon)
SIMPLETON—foolish
SINBAD—sailor, water-lover
SINCLAIR—illustrious
    (Claire)
SINNER—offensive
SIOUX—brokenhearted

SIR—respected
SIXTUS—selfish
SIZZLE—hissing, scorch
SKEETER—accurate
SKEEZER—lovable
SKIDDER—slippery
SKINNER—lean
SKIPPY—nimble
SKYLARK—musical
SLINKY—scrawny
SLIPPERY—tricky
SMARTIE—witty, clever
SMASHER—destructive
SMILEY—amusing
SMIRKY—simper
SMOKEY—hazy
SMOOCHY—affectionate
SMOOTHY—flattering
SMUDGE—blurry
SNAFU—awry
SNAPPY—flashy
SNEAKER—furtive
SNEEZY—snort
SNIFFY—supercilious
SNOOKEY—good sport
SNOOPY—inquisitive
SNOOTY—imitator
SNOOZEY—sleepy
SNOWBALL—white, silvery
   (Snowy)
SNUFF—scent
   (Snuffy)

SOAPY—smooth, flatterer
SOCORRO—helpful
SOCRATES—philosopher
SOLOMON—sunny
  (Sol, Solly)
SONNY—active, lively
SOOTY—black
SOX—comfortable, warm
SPANKY—move quickly
SPARKY—glow, kindle
SPARTACUS—fighter, gladiator
SPECK—small, bit
SPEED—fast, quick
  (Speedy)
SPELLER—magical, charmer
SPENCER—generous
  (Spenser, Spense)
SPENDER—costly
SPICY—zesty
SPIDER—long legs
SPIFFY—fine-looking, smart
SPIKE—sharp
SPINNER—twister
SPIRIT—invisible
SPLASH—scatter
SPOOK—ghost, spirit
  (Spooky)
SPORT—show-off
SPOT—dot, speck
SPRUCE—tidy, neat
SPUNKY—spirited
SPURS—energetic

SQUEAKY—shrill
STACEY—lovable
    (Stacy)
STAFFORD—watchful
STANISLAUS—warrior
    (Stanley, Stan)
STANTON—colorful
STEPHEN—victorious
    (Steven, Stefan, Steve)
STERLING—high standards
STEWART—attentive
    (Stuart, Stew, Stu)
STITCHES—sharp
STORMY—tempestuous
STREAKER —rush, swift
STREAKY—fast, rapid
STRETCH—elastic
STRIDER—progressive
STUBBORN—obstinate
STUBBY—short
SUDS—frothy
SUGAR—sweet
SUKI—tasty
SULTAN—king, sovereign
SUMNER—commanding
SUNDAY—restful
SUNSHINE—warm, optimistic
SWIFTY—quick, speedy
SYLVESTER—unselfish
    (Sy)

T

TABBY—brindled
TACKY—shabby
TACO—satisfied
TAFFY—light-colored
TAG—selective, partial
TAILSPIN—reeling, twisting
TANGLES—confused
TANGO—dancer
TANGY—spicy
TAOS—well-known
TARA—earthy
TARBABY—black
TAURUS—stubborn, the bull
TAXES—determined
TEAGUE—creative
TEDDY—protective
TEENIE—small, tiny
TEMPLETON—reformed
TERRANCE—understanding
    (Torrance, Terry)
TEWA—moccasins
TEX—water-lover
THADDEUS—helpful
    (Tad, Thad)
THEOBALD—prince
    (Theo)

THEODORE—devoted
  (Ted, Teddy)
THOMAS—a twin
  (Tom, Tommy)
THOR—roar, flashing
THUMPER—thrasher
THUNDER—explosive
THURSTON—lightning
  (Thurstan)
TIBB—trivial
  (Tibby)
TIFFY—quarrelsome
TIGER—wildcat
TIKI—supernatural
TIMOTHY—honorable
  (Tim, Timmy)
TING-A-LING—high-pitched
TIPPY—tilted
TITAN—giant
TITUS—safe
TOAD—frog
  (Toady)
TOBIAS—virtuous, even-tempered
  (Toba, Toby, Tobin)
TODD—clever, crafty
TODDY—mellow
TODY—kingfish
TONKA—unity
TOPAZ—gem, brilliant
TOPPER—uppermost
  (Toppy)
TORNADO—whirlwind

Tiger, Slinky, Bo, Fluffy

TOTTO—fuddled
  (Toto)
TOWNER—neighborly
TRACY—sketchy
TRAMP—wanderer
TRAVIS—vagabond
TREASURE—rich
TREVOR—prudent
TRIALS—skillful
TRICKY—prankster
TRINKET—trifle
TROJAN—determined
TROUBLES—worrisome
TROY—measurable
TRUE—loyal
TRUFFLES—changeable
TUBBY—pudgy, fat
  (Tubs)
TUCKER—vigorous, energetic
TUFFY—rowdy
TUMBLEWEED—bouncy
TUNICA—family man
TUSCARORA—return
TWEEDIE—chirp
TWEEDLE-DEE—musical
TWEEDLE-DUM—musical
TWEETIE—chirp
TWIG—small
TWINKLE—scintillate
  (Twinky)
TYKE—small, wee one
TYPHOON—cyclone

U

ULYSSES—king, leader
UNITY—integrity
URANUS—sunny
URIAH—hopeful
URSUS—wild ox

V

VALENTINE—valorous
    (Val)
VANCE—unselfish
VANITY—inflated
VARDEN—shepherd
VARNEY—viceroy
VAUGHN—small
VELVET—smoothie
VERE—truthful, honest
VERNON—flourishing
    (Vern)
VICTOR—conqueror
VIDA—youthful
VIGOR—active
VIKING—pirate
VIM—energetic
VINCENT—conquer
VIRGIL—flourish
VLADIMIR—prince, royal
VULCAN—fiery
VULTURE—wild bird

W

WADE—active
WADSWORTH—wanderer
WAGS—witty
WALAPAI—forester
WALDEMAN—powerful
WALDEN—mighty, powerful
    (Waldo, Wally)
WALLACE—agreeable
    (Wally)
WALTER—warrior
WANDERER—roamer
WARD—guardian
WARNER—protective
    (Vern)
WARREN—friendly
WARRICK—ruler
    (Warwick)
WARRIOR—victorious
WAYLAND—traveler
WAYNE—unselfish
WEARY—tired
WEBSTER—creative
WELLINGTON—duke
WENDELL—wandering
    (Wendel)
WERNER—prosperous
WESLEY—shepherd

WHACKY—silly, clown
WHIM—fancy, notion
WHISKERS—bristles
WHITEY—white-colored, snowy
WHITNEY—nature-lover
WHIZZER—swift, roar
WIGGLES—jerky, shaky, jiggling
WIGGLY—squirmy
WILBUR—bright, strong
WILFRED—peaceful
    (Wilfrid)
WILLARD—determined
WILLIAM—resourceful
    (Bill, Billy, Will, Willie, Willis)
WILLOUGHBY—delusive
WILMER—warrior
WINDY—stormy, breezy
WINGARD—protective
WINGY—swiftness
WINKEY—blinking
    (Winkie)
WINNEBAGO—middleman
WINSLOW—friendly
WINSTON—strong
    (Winton, Win)
WINTHROP—friendly
WIRT—worthy
WISDOM—wise
WIZARD—supernatural, charmer
WOLF—crafty
WOODROW—nature-lover
WOODY—lumberman, dense

WORRY—anxious, troubled
WYATT—dauntless
WYSTAN—immovable

X

XAVIER—brilliant
XENOPHON—strong voice
XERXES—king

Y

YARDLEY—shepherd
YATES—attentive
YAVAPAI—smiling
YOGI—philosopher
YO-YO—unwinding-rewinding
YUKIAN—prejudiced
YUMA—chief's son

Z

ZACCHEUS—devoted
   (Zachariah, Zachary, Zach, Zachy,
   Zack)
ZACHARY—thoughtful
   (Zacharias)
ZADOCK—zany
ZANDY—ridiculous
   (Zandie)
ZANE—strong
ZANY—simpleton
ZANZIBAR—unusual, mysterious
ZAPPY—electrified
ZEB—homebody
ZEKE—rigorous
ZENAS—meritorious
ZEPHYR—breezy
ZERO—lowest point
ZEUS—determined
ZIGGY—sharp
ZING—humming
ZIP—speed, vigor
   (Zippy)
ZONKY—reeling
ZORRO—accurate
ZUÑI—sleek